The Only Critter in Hamelin Town

by Michaela Morgan

Illustrated by Llewelyn Thomas

 LONGMAN

1
— By myself —

"Not now, Joseph, I'm too tired. Go and play," my mother says.

"Go and play! *WHAT* am I supposed to play? And *WHO* am I supposed to play with?" I snap.

I can answer back. I can say what I like – be as cheeky as I like. I can even swear. I could get away with anything. No one shouts at me or tells me off. They just sigh sometimes. Sometimes they cry. They drive me mad.

"How many games do you think I can play by myself? Football? By myself! Hide and seek? By myself! I'm fed up with being by myself." I slam out of the house.

Don't think I'm always bad tempered. I really try to be good, but sometimes it all gets to me. Today is one of those days. Best if I try to walk it off.

The streets are quiet as usual. A few women are coming home from the market. Each one stops and speaks to me. They smile. They ask questions. They give me sweets. They ruffle my hair. They always want to talk to me. If I fall down, I'm immediately surrounded by half a dozen grown ups, all wanting to pick me up, brush me down, kiss me better. They drive me mad.

I'm the only child you see. Not just the only child in my family, I'm the only child in the whole town. All the others were taken.

I shuffle down a side-street, kicking a stone and muttering. I don't want to be alone but I don't want to be surrounded by fussing and fretting grown ups either. I just want to be with some other kids like me. I want to play and joke and hang around with them. I can just about remember what that was like, though I haven't played with any other kids now for years.

I chip the stone into the air. *Clunk!* It hits a wall with a satisfying thump. That makes me feel a bit better. I kick more stones, harder and harder. *Clunk! Clunk! CLUNK!* The noise gets louder; the stones leap higher. Eventually, of course, they go too high, too hard and *CRRRASHH!*

That's old Mrs Slater's window. That *was* Old Slater's window anyway. Now it's a star-shaped explosion surrounded by small, diamond-sharp fragments of glass. The door opens. She comes out. I wait. In the old days you wouldn't have seen me for dust. I'd have been limping off round the corner by now, panting and trembling, surrounded by giggling and panicking kids. Now I just stand there.

"Morning, Mrs Slater," I say. "It was an accident."

" 'Course it was," says Old Slater. "You're a good boy you are. Didn't mean any harm did you?"

"No," I agree. "I was just playing."

"Playing ..." she sighs, "ah yes ... playing. Will you come in for a nice slice of cake?"

I grant her this favour to make up for the window. She's so grateful, it's pathetic – plumping up cushions all around me – cutting cake – pouring milk. All the townspeople keep a supply of cakes and sweeties in the hope of a visit from me. I would be as fat as a pig if I gave in to them all. Gran says I should make up a rota so that everyone gets a little while with me, but I never have.

"Would you like to look at some storybooks?" asks Mrs Slater. "I've got all Janie's books here, just as she left them." A sigh "... just as she left them."

"You tell me a story instead," I say. "Tell me *the* story."

"Oh ..." She doesn't really want to. I shift as if I'm thinking of leaving. It's enough of a hint. She clears her throat; she's off.

"Well, it was September time," she says, "four years ago, here in Hamelin."

"I was eight," I add.

"Eight, yes and a little weak thing you were, what with your twisted leg and all. A little scrap of a thing you were, always limping behind, shouting 'Wait for me. *Wait for me!* ' "

"And they never did."

"Well, they sometimes did but that day ..."

"Go on."

"That day ..." she shudders. "That day you were all playing ..."

"What were we playing?"

"Chasing, you know, tig and skipping – though that was mostly the girls. My little grand-daughter was always skipping. She skipped everywhere."

"What else did we play?"

"Marbles, skittles, hide and seek, football, hopscotch. Oh and such naughty things you all got up to! Playing tricks! Knocking on doors and running away and hiding. We used to get so cross with you all ..."

"It was always sunny," I say.

"Not always, Joseph, and then, of course, there were the rats."

"The rats ..." I urge. I want her to do the proper story, with the rhyme.

"And we said, 'Don't play near the rats. Stay away from the rats!' But how could you? They were everywhere. Everywhere! My Janie used to ..."

"Rats!" I want her to keep to the story. "Tell it properly – with the rhymes," I insist. And she does.

> *"Rats!*
> *They fought the dogs and killed the cats,*
> *And bit the babies in the cradles,*
> *And ate the cheeses out of the vats,*
> *And licked the soup from the cook's own ladles,*
> *Split open the kegs of salted sprats,*
> *Made nests inside men's Sunday hats,*
> *And even spoiled the women's chats*
> *By drowning their speaking*
> *With shrieking and squeaking*
> *In fifty different sharps and flats."*

"I remember," I say. "We used to throw stones at them."

"We did more than that," says Old Slater. "We put down poison, we put out traps, we blocked up their holes, tried to smoke them out but

we just couldn't get rid of them. A plague it was. A curse. How they came here no one knows."

"But we do know how they went," I say.

Mrs Slater has fallen silent. She's off in a reverie. A sad-eyed, dreamy look is on her face. She's remembering.

"Go on," I urge. "Tell the story."

"I haven't the heart," she sighs. "I feel tired all of a sudden. You just go off and play. There's a good boy. You go and play."

"Play!" I scream. "And who am I supposed to play with?"

2
— Left out —

I always felt left out. I often was left out. I was smaller, slower. I couldn't run very well. My leg was twisted and weak. I often got left behind.

"Wait for me!" I'd whine. "It's not fair. Wait for me." I wake up from dreams screaming this.

"Hush," my mother says. "It was just a dream. You've had a nightmare."

They say dreams can come true but did you know that nightmares can come true too? Mine did.

I used to dream we were all playing hide and seek. The others scattered and hid. They just vanished. Faded away. I ran from hidey place to hidey place as fast as I could. Faster and faster, as fast as I could but never fast enough, shouting, "Come out now. Come out! Come out wherever you are."

My voice starts to echo in the emptiness. No one appears and I am left standing alone, my voice echoing, wavering, growing feeble, trying not to cry as I call, "Come out. Come back. I give up. Come back ... Please!"

It was hard being different. The others called me names. They called me "Slow Joe." They called me "Wonkyleg." They called me "Hopalong." Now only grown ups call me names. They call me "Joseph dear" and "darling" and "dear little Joe" and "Son" and "Precious." My mother's always calling:

"Jo Jo! Where are you?"

"Don't go too far away!"
"Don't stay out late!"
"Be careful!"
If I stay out too long, I find her at the window staring wildly.
"It's all right, Mum," I say. "I'm here. I'm safe."
She couldn't bear to lose me too.

3
— The stranger —

Mum was waiting at the window when I got home from Mrs Slater's. She was pretending she was polishing the windows but I know she was trying to keep an eye on me.

She had tea ready. Piles of goodies and too much of everything. On either side of me stood an empty chair where my brother and sister used to sit and boss me around because I was the youngest. They used to make me eat their carrots. Then they followed the Pied Piper and I never needed to eat an extra carrot again. I would never have believed I could miss being teased and bossed, but I do.

In my bedroom (all to myself now, no need to share) I've made paintings - one of my brother waving hurry up; one of my sister smiling. It's how I remember them. In the middle I've done a huge picture of the Piper.

I remember him perfectly. He's just as they say in the story:

> *"His queer long coat from heel to head*
> *Was half of yellow and half of red;*
> *And he himself was tall and thin,*
> *With sharp blue eyes, each like a pin,*
> *And light loose hair, yet swarthy skin,*
> *No tuft on cheek, nor beard on chin,*
> *But lips where smiles went out and in –*
> *There was no guessing his kith and kin!*
> *And nobody could enough admire*
> *The tall man and his quaint attire."*

When he first came to town, we were all crazy about him. The first time I saw him he was sitting in the churchyard, dreamily playing his pipe. I was trailing along behind Peter and Martha as usual. We were supposed to be hurrying to school but we couldn't help stopping to listen. We joined the group gathered around him and listened spellbound.

The music was so sweet you could taste it.

"It's like icing!" I said to Martha. "Sugary pink and crunchy."

"More like blackberries and whipped cream," she said.

"It's gobstoppers!" said Peter. "Gobstoppers and strawberry jam!"

We all agreed we could taste the music but to each of us it tasted like our own favourite thing. Not to the grown ups though.

"I'm not one for this modern music," said the mayor. "Give me a good old-fashioned dance tune anyday."

"That's not what I call music!" said Mrs Slater. "It's nowt but wailing and squeaking."

Sometimes the music did wail, in a tone so mournful it made the heart sink and the eyes seep. Then it would soar high – a trill of high sharp notes swooping and whirling like the swifts around the church tower. And then would come some notes so deep and low that they could have come from underground.

"It really carries me away," Martha sighed and pretended to swoon.

She was wild about the Piper. She called him "dreamy". She even dressed up like him and borrowed a pipe to play. But of course she didn't get time to learn.

Martha, Peter, all the other children and the Piper are long gone now. The street that runs by the church towards Koppelberg Hill is called Pied Piper Street and there are pictures and statues of the Piper all over town. There's even a painting in the ex-mayor's office. The new mayor put it up to remind him not to make the same mistakes. There's a stained glass window in the church. Every week we pray there. We pray for forgiveness.

"Forgive us and return our children," we chant.

There's a big statue in the square. Underneath it, in black letters, is written "Lest we forget." Nobody does forget. There are songs about it, stories, poems, hymns.

I know the story by heart but I like to hear it over and over again, exactly the same. If I hear it often enough maybe one day I'll understand. I want to understand how a town full of children could just disappear. And leave me behind.

4
— Evening in Hamelin —

It's evening – quiet as usual and time for my exercises. My leg's getting stronger all the time. I hardly limp at all now. The doctor gives me lots of attention. After all, he has no other kids to look after now, does he? I have the time to do plenty of exercises. I do lift-ups, step-ups, skipping (I use my sister's old rope), I do marching and I do walking. I can walk for miles now.

The doctor says that walking uphill is the best exercise. It's more of a challenge.

"But never," he says, *"never* walk up Koppelberg Hill. You understand?"

Of course I understand. They're afraid I'll go up there and not come back – just like all the other kids.

Nevertheless, it's to Koppelberg Hill I go as often as possible and today is no exception. I have to be sneaky about it, though. Hundreds of adult eyes are always trained on me, keeping me safe, guarding me. So I set off in the opposite direction. It fools them every time. They can all see me obediently heading away from the hill.

I like to whistle or sing or chant as I march. It keeps me in step, moving quickly, picking my feet up well. I march and skip like the Piper and I march with his tune in my head, his picture in my head and the words of his story in my mouth.

> *"Into the street the Piper stepped*
> *Smiling first a little smile,*
> *As if he knew what magic slept*
> *In his quiet pipe the while;"*

I glance around. The grown ups are turning to each other, away from me. They're shaking their heads. They're wiping their eyes. I pick up speed. Then, in time to my marching, I chant:

> *"And the muttering grew to a grumbling;*
> *And the grumbling grew to a mighty rumbling;*
> *And out of the houses the rats came tumbling.*
> *Great rats, small rats, lean rats, brawny rats,*
> *Brown rats, black rats, grey rats, tawny rats,*
> *Grave old plodders, gay young friskers,*
> *Fathers, mothers, uncles, cousins,*
> *Cocking tails and pricking whiskers ..."*

One by one, grown ups are drifting indoors. Maybe they don't want to remember the day when waves of rats flowed down the street towards the big river.

> *"Families by tens and dozens,*
> *Brothers, sisters, husbands, wives –*
> *Followed the Piper for their lives,*
> *From street to street he piped advancing,*
> *And step for step they followed dancing,*
> *Until they came to the River Weser*
> *Wherein all plunged and perished"*

"And that would have been the end of it if you'd all kept your promise," I mutter. Then, quick as a rat, I skip from street to street, dodging and weaving, ducking and diving until I'm out of sight of the grown ups. With one final glance, I double back and head off for Koppelberg Hill.

5
— Koppelberg Hill —

Koppelberg Hill sticks up from Hamelin like a jagged tooth and, like a jagged tooth, I can't ignore it. You know how it is if your tooth is loose – you can't leave it alone. You have to worry at it, pushing it this way and that way, feeling the tear of the nerves, tasting the blood. It hurts but it's irresistible. That's how Koppelberg Hill is for me.

Walking up there brings the pain of the memory freshly back to me. I see all the others skipping in front of me and feel the panic rising in me as I get left further and further behind. I feel my legs shaking and stumbling again. I feel the music drawing me. The life it promises me is clear in my mind. My head is full of visions and warmth but I can't go fast enough to keep up.

"Peter!" I yell. "Martha!" and my brother and sister turn to me. Peter is waving "Hurry up." Martha is smiling. Her eyes are full of the vision. One moment they look at me and then the music draws them on and I'm left, knees grazed, legs shaking, throat burning as I sob:

"Wait for me. Wait for me!"

The music still draws me but I am left out. I am permanently left out now. Left out, let down, left behind. Why me? Wasn't I good enough? What did I do wrong? It can't be fair.

Tonight is a beautiful evening on Koppelberg Hill. Hamelin town gets smaller and smaller as I walk up higher. The air is fresh. It's the time for small animals to leave their burrows and come out for food and play. Maybe one day I'll be here and the children will leave their hollow, wherever it is, and come out and play with me. I will be able to join them.

"Halloo!" I call.

"Halloo!" my own voice echoes back.

It should be quiet up here, high, all alone, but I hear scufflings and rustlings all around me. Birds? Rabbits? Children?

The bushes around me seem to be bulging and heaving with hidden children and suppressed giggles. I hear sighs and whispers, chattering and chuckling.

From the corner of my eye I see flashes – flashes of blue eyes or dragon flies, white hair or rabbits' tails. It's difficult to be sure. They are always just out of sight, just too quick.

I feel less alone here than anywhere. I feel the others are near me. One day I will find them and join them again. I will find the land I heard of in the Piper's tune. The one I am shut out of.

One day I will catch them up. I'll hear them calling, "Joseph! Joseph come and find us!"

6
— Calling —

"JOSEPH!!"

Am I imagining it or can I hear someone calling?

I stand very still and listen.

"JOSEPH! Is that you?"

"Yes," I quaver. "Who's there?" and then I see, it's just Ben the shepherd.

He grazes his sheep up here - and looks for his son Max and little Rosie, his daughter.

"Joseph! What are you doing up here?" He's got hold of my shoulder.

"Exercising my leg," I say. "Marching and climbing."

"Well, you can just go marching and climbing down to the town again," he says. "This is no place for young 'uns."

'This is the only place for young 'uns,' I think. 'All the young 'uns are here.'

"I thought I heard whispering," I say, "and giggling. Listen!"

He cocks his head to one side and concentrates fiercely.

"Wind," he says. "Leaves rustling and a stream somewhere babbling. That's what it is."

"But I thought I saw ..."

"I know, lad. Many's the time I think I catch a glimpse of my Rosie and Max but it's just tricks of the light. 'Tain't possibly them after all this time and all that searching. A trick of the light. A trick of hope. Best forgotten."

"I can't forget," I say, "and I don't want to."

"Ah lad, I understand. Come on, I'll walk down with you. Does no good to hang around up here, worrying and imagining. 'Tis too late to do anything about it now but I tell you if I had my time again and I'd made a promise, I'd think twice about breaking it."

"Why couldn't you all have just kept your word and paid the Piper what he asked?" It's not the first time I've asked this question.

"Do you think we don't ask ourselves that – every waking day? Do you not think we wished we'd kept our word? Do you not think we'd do anything to undo the wrong we did? But we're just human, boy, we make mistakes. We don't always see so clear."

He sits on a rock and gazes down at the town.

"From this distance it looks different but when you're in there ... We didn't really believe in him, you know. So we agreed to give him everything he asked for. We didn't really believe he could rid the town of rats. We were just desperate. Then, when he did it, we all went a bit wild like.

"Flabbergasted we were. And the celebrating we did – the parties, the drinking – well it fair fuddled the brain. Why, we'd all but forgot about the Piper, what with the bells ringing and the singing and the dancing – for days it went on. Flummoxed we were. Then up he pops and 'One thousand guilders,' says he, 'as agreed'.

"Then we all gets to thinking. 'One thousand guilders is a terrible lot. Won't ye take less?' we say. After all, who's to say 'twas he who got the rats to jump in the river? Mebbe they just took it into their heads to do it like those ...'"

"Lemmings?" I suggest.

"Aye, like lemmings. We couldn't believe he'd done it. We don't generally think much of magic round these parts."

"You should never break a promise," I say. "Never."

"Well lad, you're right. And we were wrong. Mean we were. A debt not paid, a promise broken and if we could make up for it ..."

He looks so downhearted, slumped on his rock gazing at the town. "Come on, Ben," I say. "We've got to go back now. It's getting dark."

7
— Storytime —

My mum was waiting at the door. My dad was out looking for me.

"You're five minutes late," she snapped but she hugged me at the same time. If she'd known I'd been up Koppelberg Hill, she'd have been in fits.

Ben wouldn't tell on me. I'd made him promise. They think twice before breaking promises to kids nowadays.

I went straight up to bed, good as gold. Then, "Storytime," I call. Mum tried all the usual tricks.

"I'm a bit busy dear."

"It's too late."

But I don't let her off, even when she gets desperate.

"You're too old for stories," she tries.

And then, "Why do you want that same story over and over again?"

"Because it's true!" I scream. "I need it."

She sighs and sits down.

"Where shall I start?" she asks.

"After he got rid of the rats," I say.

Her face is white, her lips pinched.

"He got rid of the rats," she says.

"Yes," I say "and the grown ups broke their promise."

"Yes," she agrees wearily. "We let him down."

"Betrayed him."

"Yes ..."

"So then?"

She's silent.

"Tell me again. The same way. The same words. Again."
A sigh, then she begins:

> *"Once more he stepped into the street;*
> *And to his lips again*
> *Laid his long pipe of smooth sweet cane ..."*

She starts garbling it, trying to get it over quickly.
"Tell it properly," I insist. "Please, Mum."
I help her out by joining in:

> *"There was a rustling, that seemed like a bustling*
> *Of merry crowds justling at pitching and hustling.*
> *Small feet were pattering, wooden shoes clattering,*
> *Little hands clapping and little tongues chattering ..."*

She sniffs and wipes a hand across her face.

> *"And, like fowls in a farmyard when barley is scattering,*
> *Out came the children running ..."*

"I'm back," shouts my dad from downstairs. "Everything all right?"
"Yes, Jack," shouts my mum. "He turned up just after you left. He's in bed now but Jack ..."
"Yes?"
"Do you think you could finish the story for me, I don't feel ..."
"That nonsense again!" he roars and he's up the stairs in three bounds.

"Listen here, Joe, you're nearly twelve. What do you want with story-telling at your age, eh? What do you want with *that* story over and over again. What's the good of it?"

"I said I would," says Mum quietly. "I promised. You go and have your supper, Jack. I'll do it."

He stomps off. I give her a little smile. I think she understands. I think sometimes she needs to keep going over it too. She goes to all the ceremonies, the prayer meetings. She holds my hand and starts:

> *"The mayor was dumb, and the council stood*
> *As if they were changed into blocks of wood,*
> *Unable to move a step, or cry*
> *To the children merrily skipping by ..."*

"Peter and Martha and you too," she adds. "Just stood up and left the house. 'Where do you think you're off to?' I said and you all turned and your eyes were all dreamy as if you were drifting away and off you skipped. Peter and Martha and you trailing behind and the streets full of skipping dream-eyed children and staring, helpless adults. And you all skipping towards the river, just like the rats. 'He's never going to drown them too, is he?' says the mayor.

"And the sigh – the relief – when he turned you all away from the river and towards the hill. 'He'll not get them to climb all the way up there,' we thought. 'He can't climb and pipe. They'll have to stop soon. They'll have to stop ...' "

She's off in her own world now, so I finish the story for her:

"When, lo, as they reached the mountain's side,
A wondrous portal opened wide,
As if a cavern was suddenly hollowed;
And the Piper advanced and the children followed
And when ..."

"That's enough!!" shouts Dad. Back up the stairs he bounds. "What's the point of all this? You should forget."

But I carry on:

> *"And when all were in to the very last,*
> *The door in the mountain side shut fast,"*

"Stop right now and go to sleep or I'll ..."

> *"Did I say all? No! one was lame ..."*

"Joseph, Joseph where's the good in this?" He's almost crying.

> *"And could not dance the whole of the way;*
> *And in after years, if you would blame*
> *His sadness, he was used to say,*
> *'It's dull in our town since my playmates left!*
> *I can't forget that I'm bereft ...'"*

I'm crying now too and can't carry on.

> *"I can't forget ..."*

"Shush, Joseph. Shush now," says my mum. "Try to sleep. Shush."

8
— Baking day —

The next morning is hot. It's a little airless as if a storm may be brewing. Mum is up early, clattering in the kitchen. It's baking day.

"Now, where did I put it?" she mutters. "Have you seen the big cake tin? You haven't been using it for one of your games have you?"

"Why do you want *that* one?" I say. "Use one of the others." But I know what she's up to. It's my birthday soon and she wants to make a special cake. The bag on top of the wardrobe is beginning to bulge with suspicious lumps. The presents have started to arrive. Everyone in the town sends a present and my mum tries to hide them until the day. She has a hard time. So many presents arrive, she runs out of hiding places! I like to tease her about it.

"Shall I fetch some wood before I go out?" I ask, looking innocent but knowing full well the log shed is packed with hidden presents.

"Oh no, Joe, don't worry about that now," says Mum, unsuspicious. "You can just play."

"Can I play in the barn?" I tease. The barn is another of her hiding places.

"On second thoughts," Mum panics, "perhaps you could go to the market for me."

" 'Course," I say. "Shall I take the big shopping bag from the top of the wardrobe?"

I've gone a bit too far. She realises she's been rumbled.

"You rascal! You've been having me on," she laughs and pretends to swipe one floury hand at me. "Be off with you!" She's humming with happiness now. She loves baking and making things for me.

"You could pick up some vegetables from the market while you're out," she adds. "And think about what you'd like from me and Dad for your birthday. Something special that you'd really like, eh? Your dad and I have racked our brains and we couldn't think of a thing! You just tell us what you want and we promise to get it!"

I can imagine them fretting about how they can make me happy. What can they give that someone else hasn't already got for me. They are always trying so hard as though, if they could just get it right, they could make up for everything.

I give her a hug.

"I can't think of any present I haven't already got at least two of. But I'll try to think of something special that only you can give."

I get a floury pat and a kiss and then the familiar anxiety crosses her face.

"Now, where are you going? How long will you be?" She's off!

"I'm going to the market for you, remember," I answer. "Then I'll hang around the market square for a bit, maybe have a drink or an ice cream. I'll be an hour, couple of hours at the most."

"There's the list and the money. Now, you'll be careful, won't you?"

"Yes, Mum."

"You won't go near the hill?"

"No, Mum."

"Or the river?"

"No, Mum."

"You won't be late back?"

"Oh give it a rest, Mum."

I feel sorry as soon as I've said it. She looks so hurt. She tries so hard to make everything better for me but her fussing drives me mad.

"Sorry," I mumble, grab the bag and set off for the market. "Back in a couple of hours. Don't worry."

" 'Bye," she waves. "Have fun and try to think what we can get for your birthday."

9
— Market —

The market is crowded and colourful. Everyone notices me, greets me, questions me.

"Where are you off to, Joseph?"

"Helping your mum are you, Joe?"

"My! How you've grown!"

"Look how well he walks now! Hasn't he done well!"

Some questions are attempts to find out my size, my likes and dislikes. They are fishing for clues, trying to find out what will make a good birthday present.

"Look how big you are, Joseph! What size of shoes do you take now?"

They think I don't know what they are up to and I don't like to disappoint them so I pretend innocence. I play along with them and

feed them with the hints and information they need to get their gifts just right.

It's a relief to talk to the market traders. They treat me normally.

"Get your mucky hands off those tomatoes!" one of them says. They come from the surrounding towns, so the sight of a child is nothing special to them. They are gruff with me. Offhand. They tease me and tell me off. It's great. It makes me feel normal.

Once one of them brought her baby daughter with her. Everyone soon made her realise her mistake – shrieks of delight at seeing a baby, mixed with screams of fear and warnings.

"Get her out of town quickly!"

"Save her before she's disappeared like our poor children!"

"Hurry, dear. Take her back to your town. It isn't safe for children here. Haven't you heard the story?"

She must have been new to the area. Everyone knows our story. Strangers stare at me and whisper.

"That's the one that wasn't taken. The only one left."

It looks like I'll always be the only one. People with children don't come to live in Hamelin. If a new baby is born in town, it's not long before its parents suddenly decide to move to a new area. I remember the Millers. Mr Miller was determined to stay.

"I'm not afraid," he said. "This is my home, and here we stay."

But Mrs Miller grew more and more nervous as the days passed. If she saw a flash of colour, she gasped and ran to check that her baby was still in its cot. If a stranger came to town, she clutched her baby and hid. She became afraid to leave the house. Then, one day she heard a snatch of music and she locked herself and the baby in the house and screamed and screamed and screamed.

By the end of the week they'd moved out.

10
— A special present —

Shopping done, I lean back against the fountain in the market place. I'm soaking in the late autumn sun, the sounds, the scents, and I'm thinking,

"What *would* I like for my birthday?"

The market is full of shirts and shoes and toys I wouldn't mind having but, from the whisperings and nudgings that surround me whenever I stop to look at something, I know the townspeople are all ready to get these for me. I have to be really careful – anything they think I'm interested in, they get for me. This can lead to some difficult situations. Perhaps I would just stop to look at something because I thought it was so hideous. Next thing I know, some well-meaning person is smiling and pressing it into my hands and I'm unwrapping it and pretending to be delighted.

I don't like to hurt their feelings but their generosity knows no bounds. If I say "Aaah" when I see a puppy, I can bet the puppy will turn up as a gift. If I pat a rabbit, a rabbit I will get. Once I paused to look at a donkey and now I have a donkey. Mum says our garden is getting more like a zoo every day. Today a man came through the town with a herd of lop-eared goats. They stared at me with eyes like marbles. I wanted to feed one but didn't dare. My mum would have a blue fit if a herd of goats turned up as a birthday present.

I drift into a dream of bicycles and books but, back home, I have enough stuff to keep me busy for another twelve birthdays. What would I really like? I already have everything – except friends, of course. *Of course!* That's what I'd like for my birthday. I know that no children will be allowed to *stay* in this town but could they come for a party? Just a short party!

Imagine it! Someone to show all my presents to. Someone to play and talk with, if only for an afternoon. Yes! That's it! A birthday party! That's what I'll ask for.

11
— Another promise —

"A birthday party!" says my mum in horror. "How?!"

"Have a bit of sense, lad," says Dad. "You know folk won't allow their young 'uns to hang around Hamelin."

"But it'll just be for an hour or two, Dad. Where's the harm in that?"

"I don't know ..." says Mum. "I suppose we could send you away to another town for your party?"

"But that's not what I want. I want everyone to come here. I want them to play with my things, look at my pets, come to see *me*. None of my things have ever been played with except by me. I want to try them out with other kids. I want to show them how well I can do with my things. It won't be for long, Mum. What can happen in an hour or two?"

"Well ..."
     "It's years since the disappearing now. Nothing's happened to me in all these years. It's about time everyone stopped being frightened."
     "Hmmm ..."

"And ..." my final argument, "you did say I could have *anything*. Remember, you promised."

So the invitations went out.

12
— Preparation —

The following days seemed to fly by. I checked through all my things, selecting games and toys I thought would be good for the party day. I put my puppy through his tricks. Those other kids would be so impressed when they saw how well I'd trained him! I'd spent hours with him. He could shake hands, play dead - all the usual tricks. Plus, I'd built a course for him - tunnels to go through, and planks to balance on, barrels and fences to jump. He was brilliant at it. I couldn't wait to show him off to some other kids.

I spent one day brushing the donkey in case anyone wanted to ride him. He looked as shiny as a conker.

Mum and Dad went into a flurry of housework and a panic of organisation - borrowing extra chairs and a long table, cooking and baking, getting everything ready.

"It'll be a grand day," said Old Ben. "If they come."

"They will," I said "... well, some of them will. Some have made excuses of course. Cowards! They're visiting aunts or going on holiday or performing in concerts all of a sudden. But my mum says she's written and explained to all my cousins and they've definitely promised to come. All the townsfolk have asked their relatives' and friends' kids too. We've sent out so many invitations - some are bound to come, aren't they?"

"Hope so," said Ben. "Certainly hope so."

"I can't wait," I confided, "and do you know what the best thing of all will be?"

"What?"

"When they come and find it's all right. When their dads and mums realise it's safe ... and when the kids see all my things and meet me and get to like me, you know what?"

"What?"

"They'll come again. They'll like it ... they'll like *me* so much that they'll want to come again. I'll have friends!"

"Aye, and then they'll open the school again," said Ben, twinkling. "Won't *that* be a treat for you!"

"It'll be worth it," I say. "And, anyway, I'm fed up with having lessons all by myself – just me and the minister! I really have the feeling things are going to change. I can feel it."

"Aye," said Ben. "There's a scent of change in the air."

He watched me tickling the ears of a sheep.

"Taken a fancy to that sheep have you?"

Oh no! I could guess that another present was coming my way!

13
— Autumn —

The evenings were getting darker. Autumn was in the air but there was still a spring in my step as I took my evening exercise up Koppelberg Hill. I was marching to songs and dreams of party games. I was imagining the other children gathering round me, admiring my presents; gathering round me, singing. Imagine children gathering round me! It made me feel light and warm to think of being surrounded, accepted, a part of something. To think of singing with others, playing with others, laughing with others.

"HAA AAA AAA AAAA," a laugh. I heard a laugh! But it wasn't a pleasant one. Bitter it sounded. Harsh. Raucous.

"HAAA AAA AAAA!"

There was no one in sight. It must be the disappeared children. Underground they were and laughing. They were laughing at me. Mocking me and my plans.

"You think I can't do it, do you?" I shout. "You think I'm not good enough? You think because you didn't want me no one else will!"

"HAAA AAA AAA!"

"Stop it! You're not the only children in the world you know."

"HAAA AAAA AAA!" Long and harsh, a rasping laugh. A hideous cackle of a laugh.

"Well, I've got news for you." I'm shaking. "Children, *dozens* of them, are coming to see me - specially to see me! So, what do you think of that?"

"HAAAAAA AAAAA AAAAAAAA" – getting louder, nearer.

"Come out and show yourselves," I yell. "Come out here! Come out! Come out wherever you are."

The rasping noise grew louder – *"HA AAAA AAAA!"* Harsher, nearer, and then the cackling laughter sound mixed with the sound of wings as a flock of honking wild geese flew over my head.

The sound vanished with them as they disappeared into the distance. I stood there, foolish and alone, as they faded out of sight.

14
— Party day —

The day of my birthday dawned clear and bright.

I spent a long time unwrapping presents and thanking everyone.

"Shoes! Thank you – and they're just the right size!"

"The shirt I liked. Thank you."

"Oh, a sheep, Ben! What a surprise."

They stand over me, smiling and anxious. They lap up my thanks and my feigned surprise. One thing I'm not pretending is my excitement about the party. As the time draws near, the house buzzes and hums like a hive. Bustling this way and that are folk bringing and arranging the party. Cakes and apple juice, cream and pies, ham and cheeses and lines of little gifts; one for each of my new friends to take home. I bet they don't get the chance to come to many parties like this! I get myself ready in good time and stand and wait by the window, stiff in my new clothes, a huge smile stretched across my face, my eyes and ears alert for the sound of the guests arriving. My heart and my stomach are fluttering with a mixture of hope and nerves and happiness.

I'm still standing there two hours later but now my stomach and heart are heavy. Dead weights. Tiredness drains me. My jaws ache from the smiling.

The bustling in the background has slowly silenced and now the grown ups stand and look shifty. One by one they start to drift away.

"I'm sorry, Joseph," says Old Slater. "They did say they'd come. They must have lost heart at the last minute."

"Don't take it too hard," says my dad. "There'll be other birthdays."

My mum pats my arm and starts clearing away the untouched party. She moves stiffly, as noiselessly as possible.

Ben's gone too.

"Try to forgive them lad," he'd said. "Try to understand."

I do understand. I understand things will not change for me. Day will follow day here in Hamelin with me buried alive by loneliness and fear ...

My throat is tight. I feel as if I have a huge lump of undigested bread stuck in my gullet. I pull off my new tie, rip open the collar of the new shirt.

"Going for a walk," I manage to say. I'm choking with uncried tears. Suffocating in fallen hopes.

"Where ..." My Mum's off again.

"Koppelberg Hill!" I spit the words out and, quick as a rat, I'm gone.

15
— Bereft —

I start by running as fast as I can – faster than I can. I want the tight band around my heart to loosen. I'm soon tiring and I end by staggering, shaky-legged, dizzy-headed. My knees are scraped from falls, my heart is pounding. I feel sick with disappointment. I feel as I did on the day of the disappearing, all that time ago.

"It's not fair," I announce to the hill. "The stupid, stupid cowards. They let me down again. They'd *promised!*"

It's people who are the real rats and Hamelin is still plagued. I lie on the ground and sob. Heaving, racking, painful sobs that seem to come from very deep within me.

I have never cried so much in my life. Not even on that day when I was left behind. I feel as if I have rivers of tears to shed. Oceans of them. They come like the tide, huge and heaving, powerful, relentless. They wash me along and all the pain, all the loneliness, all the bitterness I've ever choked back wells up in me, pours out and spills into the grass of Koppelberg Hill.

The sun is starting to go down by the time I am drained of tears. I'm exhausted now, half awake, half asleep. I seem to drift in and out of consciousness until, finally, I slide down, down, down into a deep dreamless sleep. I feel myself falling ... falling.

Much later, I wake and feel as a tree must feel after a storm – battered but somehow refreshed, washed out and washed clean. I feel emptied and clean and transformed. I sit and stare. Everything looks clear and new and different. Hamelin town, down in the valley, is so small, huddled up in the hollow and I am up here floating above it. Free of it ...

What is there in Hamelin for me? Another day and another and another, each like the one before, long and dreary. Another day of being fed and patted like a prize poodle. Another day of smiling and pretending, racing against shadows, talking to stones. Listening to old folk muffled by fear and superstition.

I feel emptied. Empty of Hamelin, emptied of hope. I remember the dreams the Piper's music filled me with and the promises it made to me. Then I catch a glimpse of something at the edge of my vision. Something scuttling in a bush?

"Follow, follow," says a voice. Or is it a bird, "Cuckoo, cuckoo"?

"Here, here," someone whispers. Or is it the wind and the leaves? I can hear and see so much clearer, as if my tears have washed my senses. Gigglings I hear and gurglings. Colours – so bright, so clear! The sky so blue! So cloudless! And now there's a rainbow, a rainbow flashing over me, its many colours fragile and beautiful. It falls on me.

"Where does the rainbow end?" I used to wonder. Now I know – it ends at me. I am at the end of the rainbow, bathed in all its colours. I lie back and soak them in. I close my eyes and let the colour sink into me, engulf me. I'm merging. Dissolving. Blending. Falling ... falling. Falling, fading, floating. Soaking through grass, fading through flowers, merging with the mountain. It's accepting me.

16
— Inside —

Back in Hamelin by now the party is packed away. The chairs and the long table are returned to their owners, the presents arranged or put away. The sheep is in the garden, the grown ups in their chairs, waiting and watching for me, looking up to Koppelberg Hill, willing me to come down. Maybe some of them are up on the hill looking for me.

"Joseph ... Joseph" are they calling? "Joseph, come back. Come here. Come out ..."

And me? Where am I?

I'm lying in some soft, mossy place. I feel safe. I feel surrounded. I feel *inside*. It's warm. Like lying in a bath - warmth lapping around me, surrounding me. A sense of peace.

I can see very little. I am used to the harsher light outside. Here it is a twilight glow, soft, half-dark. I lie and listen. All sounds are strangely muffled. A distant whooshing of water, music faint in the air and also, in the distance, the sound of children playing.

"Come and find me! Come and find me!" I hear snatches of songs, distant laughter.

I am with the disappeared. I am one of them now. I have been taken in too.

17
— Joining in —

I move towards the sounds. Strangely, I don't run. Dreamlike, I am in the half-light. Calm. My head is full of clouds, muffled. The noise is sweet. There is laughter and singing, gentle and subdued. It's not the wild whooping, fighting and scrapping, shriekings and clatterings that I remember from the old days.

The passage widens and I'm looking down into a huge underground valley with soft cloud-bank sides. At the bottom there's a stream sparkling, trees waving – and dozens and dozens of children.

Some are kneeling, playing marbles. Some are sitting, chattering, giggling. Some are floating small bark boats in the stream. A large group is skipping. At each end of a huge rope one child keeps time, turning the rope in perfect slow and steady rhythm.

"*Flip flap, flip flap.*" One by one, children are jumping in, taking their place in the rope. They all seem to be wearing rainbows.

I move towards them. I put a foot onto the cloud bank side, leading down to the valley. It's like walking in thick snow – a slow sinking, dissolving. I sink towards the children playing in the valley. I listen to them chant as they skip.

> *"The flowers are singing,*
> *The sun is singing,*
> *The water is singing,*
> *And so am I."*

I seem to know this song somehow. Was it part of the Piper's music? I watch the rope going up and down, up and down. I see the children, singing, waiting for the right moment to jump in and join the line of skippers. I am absorbed by the rhythm. I join in with the words.

> *"The colours join in.*
> *The clouds join in.*
> *The trees join in.*
> *And so do I."*

I jump in. In perfect time, I jump up and down with the others. In harmony I sing.

> *"Sun*
> *Water*
> *Sky*
> *Me"*

> *"Earth*
> *Air*
> *Fire*
> *Me"*

Here I am. One of them.

I look down the line of children jumping up and down, up and down. At last I am one of them, the same as them. Then I notice something. How big I am ... I - I who was always called "titchy" and "weedy" - seem to have outgrown them.

18
— Reunion —

I see Janie Slater skipping. She looks the same as on the day she disappeared four years ago. She's got the same blue eyes, blonde hair, smiling face. A small, skippy person, sunny and smiley. Not one day older.

There are little Rosie and Max, just as I remember them. Rosie, pink and dimpled, skipping and singing. Max, thin and serious watching from the side. And there are Jacob and Mary and Will and John and Alice and Daisy and Rebecca, Rachel and Sarah and Tom and Rob. And there's Martha – and Peter. They are sitting on a grassy mound, waving to me, still waving as they were all those years ago. They don't seem at all surprised to see me.

"Hey, Joseph! Come on over here!" they call.

I wave back. I feel stunned, slowed down as if in a dream. There is too much to take in. I move towards them. It's more like swimming than walking – an effortless, floaty drifting. They act as if only half a minute has passed since they last saw me. I go right up to them. Peter, who always seemed so huge and strong to me. Peter, who could knock me to the floor with one tickle. Peter, who could wrestle any toy away from me. I'm as big as Peter now. Martha, always so big and bossy. Martha, who could make me do whatever she wanted, stands up. I can look down on her. They glance at each other as if wondering how this came about but they are soon caught up in their game again. Singing, chanting, running, tumbling – they ask no questions.

"Come and play with us," they say.

How long I have been waiting to hear someone say that!

19
— Recreation —

Football, bulldogs, leapfrog, hopscotch ... time passed. Tig and tag, hide and seek, marbles ... time passed. Chasing, racing, swinging, singing ... How much time? I don't know. It could have been hours. It could have been months. It was like the old days at school when the teachers let us out for recreation. Only here no one ever rang a bell to tell us to stop. It was forever playtime.

"You know," I said to Max, "I was really looking forward to my birthday party. It was my last hope. But this ... this is a million times better than I could have imagined." And it was. For here I was among all the children who'd left me behind. The ones who'd called me little and slow and now I was as good as them - better. I was bigger than many. Quicker than most. I won game after game and no one seemed to mind. They would just smile and drift off to the next game.

"What shall we play now?" The other children would gather round me. "Show us a new game!"
I had the best ideas for games. I had more or less the only ideas. Instead of being Slow Joe, tagging on, begging to be included, whining at being left out, I became Joseph, the leader, the organiser, the first, the best.

When we've played enough, we sit and sing. We sit on the ground. Above us little lights (fireflies? stars?) twinkle. There is an evening feel. Rosie starts to sing in her clear, high voice:

> *"He is all colours,*
> *All colours he.*
> *He came for us.*
> *He set us free."*

We all join in and sing in a round:

> *"All colours.*
> *All colours he.*
> *He came, he came.*
> *He set us free."*

Repeated and repeated, lulling like waves lapping around me. One by one, we fall asleep.

20
— Dream life —

When the next 'morning' comes, we eat. Fruit appears on trees. We pick and eat it. There is always more fruit. It never runs out. It never goes out of season.

A table under the trees is always laid – never in disarray. It is permanently laid with creamy-fresh, bubbly milk (but where are the cows?). So fresh and bubbly it must just have been poured (but who poured it?). There are sweets and cakes – piles of them, mountains of them. Chocolate lies thick as a ploughed field. It never melts or goes sticky.

There is always cheese and meat and honey. There is always bread. The bread is always crusty and fresh. Everything is there for us. Always there.

This seemed mysterious to me but, gradually, I did come to accept it. The other children never doubted or wondered. They believed that everything was for the best and this was the best of all worlds.

"Where's the Piper?" I asked once.

"Around ..." they said vaguely. But there is no sign of the Piper. All that remains is a hint of music in the air. It's faint, almost imperceptible but it fills the head with clouds. It's always at the back of the ears, ready to swell into life. No one except me misses the sounds of the world – the birdsong or the bleating of sheep that should surround us. No one asks questions.

"Don't you wonder why I've grown so much and you haven't?" I ask. But no, they didn't wonder.

"Don't you wonder why I can walk so well now?" I ask. But no, they didn't wonder.

In fact, I wasn't running, marching or walking nowadays anyway. I drifted. Life was slow and sweet. Mouth filled with sweets, ears filled with music, head filled with clouds, I felt myself turning dreamy, vague.

"I need an adventure," I thought. I had to shake my head to think – like a dog that comes out of the water, ears filled with wet and weed.

"Let's explore out of the valley," I suggested.

A few gazed up at the cloud-bank hills, but ...

"No."

"Too far ..."

"Why should we?"

"Everything we need is here ..." and they drifted back to their chanting, skipping and playing.

21

— Memories —

I go anyway. I've never been the sort of person who gives up easily. If I could get up Koppelberg Hill, I could climb up the sides of this valley!

"What's the point?" asks Max. "Stay here and have an ice cream." He holds the creamy yellow cone just out of my reach. "Do you want it?" but I choose to go. It reminds me of sneaking up Koppelberg Hill. Although no one has forbidden me to climb this hill, it feels forbidden. It also feels difficult.

Up, up, up. Very soon my legs are aching and I don't seem to have made any progress. Am I losing my strength?

Up, up, up.

I look down and see Max laughing at me.

"You can't do it. Just give up. We've started a game of football. Come on, play with us," he waves me down.

It would be so easy to slip down and join him. He waves the ball temptingly but I carry on trying to climb and soon he wanders off and starts playing with someone else. I hear them laughing – at me?

One step, two steps, three ... but I still seem to be in the same place. It's like climbing a cloud of cotton wool. Banks of clouds, frothy and insubstantial as snow or candy floss – there's nothing to get hold of. I seem to sink in. I can't move forward and, worse, every time I rest or look down, I seem to sink and slide back down to the beginning. It's like those dreams of running. Running, running, running and never getting anywhere.

I'm exhausted by effort, frustration and disappointment. I lie at the bottom of the cloud bank and close my eyes. All my muscles are aching. My brain is too. Why couldn't I climb up?

I remembered the first times I'd tried to climb up Koppelberg Hill. Those times had been terrible too. My leg was still weak and twisted. I had to drag it along behind me. At times, I was so exhausted I had practically to crawl, feeling sick and dizzy with the effort. But even on the worst days, when I was pulling myself up by clumps of grass, my knuckles skinned, my knees scraped, there had been wonderful moments – when I lay panting and still and weak and a rabbit would pop up and twitch its nose at me. Or a lark would rise, its song sweet and sharp. Or a snake would slither swiftly away to hide. I felt blessed to see such things. My spirits lifted at these memories and I sat up at the bottom of the cloud bank. I gathered the remnants of my strength together and began the cloud climb again.

I pick one heavy, aching leg up and move it forward. What an effort! Oh, it reminds me so much of those early attempts to climb Koppelberg. At one time the doctor had strapped my leg inside a special support made of wood and leather. It was to hold my leg straight. It hurt and it was heavy. At first, I'd had to pick my leg up with my arms when I wanted to move it but the weight and the pain had been worth it. Bit by bit, my leg grew stronger and straighter.

My head is full of these Hamelin memories when, suddenly - a shock! I feel a surge of movement and, somehow, I've moved up the cloud bank. I've got higher. I'm so surprised that I slip back a bit but I have still made progress!

I feel elated by these little steps full of hope and power.

22
— Climbing through clouds —

After that, I returned regularly to my climbing. At first I slid and stumbled and staggered. Now I walk easily. I stretch my legs and hold my head high. I feel as if I am exercising my body and my mind and my memories.

I have discovered that I can only move up the valley when my head is full of the life overground. These memories seem to block the Piper's music, which can hold me like a magnet, so I fill my head with thoughts of home and Hamelin. I drown out the Piper's music by singing Hamelin hymns and songs and stories. I think of the hill above me and the streets, the houses, the road to my house ... My house! I can see it in my mind. I can see my mother at the window, watching. Today I feel higher than ever before.

Below me the children, fluttering and multi-coloured, shimmying here and there, look like butterflies.

My head feels so much clearer up here. It reminds me of the fresh evening air on Koppelberg Hill.

I sit in between the overground and the underground and I wonder, "Where do I belong? Where do I want to be?" For the first time, it seems to me that I have a choice.

23

"Look at you!" Max says. "You've ripped your clothes and your shoes are full of clouds. What a mess!"

"And your head is full of clouds," I reply. "Have you any idea what you look like?"

Now that I can see things from a different angle, I've started to notice how pale the other children are. They are whitefaced and ghostlike. They remind me more and more of the sad Hamelin folk, subdued, half dead and half alive.

"Don't you ever wonder how things are in Hamelin?" I ask the others. But no, they don't ever think of it.

"Hamelin ..." says Peter, dreamily, "Hamelin?"

I sometimes talk of Hamelin, of home. I sing Hamelin songs and tell Hamelin stories.

"Don't you remember the rats?" I ask.

"The rats?" Peter looks confused.

"How they ran through the church that day and ran up the minister's sleeve ... How everyone screamed and fell on top of each other, running to get out – and Mrs Slater, Janie's gran, fell in the font! What a splash she made!

"Don't you remember the nests they made! The gutters they blocked! The waterfalls they caused! How they nested in the mayor's best hat. His face went purple!"

Many children have gathered to listen now. They are giggling. They like my stories.

"One day they got into school during the spelling test and we were let off! And once they got into the church tower and up the bell rope. The bells clanged day and night! No one could guess who was ringing at first. Some thought it was ghosts but we found rats swinging and gnawing at the ropes. They were everywhere. They started a stampede of cows through the market place once. Don't you remember? They sent everything scattering – animals, apples, cabbages and people! There were chickens in the cream, sheep in the cheese, goats eating the flower stall!" Peter is laughing. His cheeks are going pink.

"I remember now!" he says. "I think I remember ..."

"Yes," I said. "You must remember. Mum would shriek. Every time she opened a cupboard, there would be a set of whiskers twitching, a pair of eyes staring."

"I remember now," said Martha, shuddering in fear.

"And the noise! Don't you remember the noise? The shriekings and squeakings ..."

"I don't remember any of that. You're making it up," says Max. "Don't listen to his silly stories." He starts to lead Rosie away.

"You must remember the time the rats surrounded your flock?" I insist. "Waves of rats came, like a grey greasy sea all around your sheep. They went for the new-born lambs – ripped their throats and eyes. Ben, your dad, was in such a state. Shaking he was, and shouting, running this way and that, trying to protect his poor lambs. Their mothers were wild-eyed and stamping ... and the wailing and the bleating and the smell of blood and panic ... how we couldn't do anything to stop it."

"I remember," says Rosie. "I remember. I hate them!" Anger and tears rush through her face, turning it bright red. "Oh, I remember now!"

24
— Stories —

This started a habit. Every now and then someone would come up to me.

"Tell us a story," they'd say.

Sometimes I told them the same story over and over, sometimes a new one, a wildly made-up one or a true one. I became the storyteller. While they'd all been wrapped up in the earth, tucked up and warm, I'd been outside. I'd heard stories. I'd seen things.

"Tell us a story," they chorus.

"Which one today?" I ask.

"A story about princesses?" I suggest to Janie (she likes those ones). "Or dragons? Ghosts? Battles?"

"Tell us a story about a brother and sister," says Rosie, snuggling into Max's side. "Do you know one of those?"

"Let me think ... Oh yes, the story of Hansel and Gretel who were left all alone, abandoned in the woods."

"How?"

"Why?"

"Their parents were very poor. They didn't know how to cope so they ... lost their children."

A muttering of angry voices at this. My storytelling sessions were really waking them up.

"What happened to the children?" asks Rosie.

"They wandered in the woods ... lost in the woods, deep and dark, for a long time. Cold they were, alone and hungry and very very afraid."

Rosie shudders and snuggles into Max.

"Then one day they came to a clearing in the woods. Sunny and bright it was. And in the middle of the clearing, what do you think they saw? A little house! A sweet little house. A very sweet house. It was made of sweets!"

"Ooh!"

"Gingerbread door and liquorice chimney, spun-sugar windows and candyfloss curtains. A very sweet little house ..."

"Yum!" says Tom.

"The children were half starved and to see so many sweets and to feel so much light and colour after their time in the dark wood was ... well, it fair took their breath away. They licked the latch. They nibbled the windows. They chewed the chimney. Then they set to scoffing the front door. Then up pops a strange figure – a strange little old woman.

" 'Come in my dears,' says she 'Come on in and be comfortable.' "

Rosie has fallen asleep, sucking her thumb.

"I'll carry on tomorrow," I say to the others. They groan and complain. This isn't like them. When I arrived, they smiled and accepted everything! Still, they don't keep it up for long.

"That's just the way it is!" I grin. "You don't get everything all at once!"

25
— In between worlds —

After storytelling sessions now I often sneak off to climb up the cloud banks. Up I go, surefooted as a mountain goat. It's wonderful! The air is clear and fresh and I feel clear and fresh too. I feel as if I am stretching myself after a long, warm, curled-up time in bed. Up here I sit and look down on the children playing. I have that same feeling of in-between-ness I'd felt on Koppelberg Hill; as if I don't completely belong.

I think back to Hamelin, to the time of the rats and the long long time I spent as the only child in a world of grown ups. I remember feeling as if my life was invaded, overrun by busybody adults. I remember the way they nagged, the way they teased and I remember the way they broke their promises. I feel a surge of anger. I'm glad if they're missing us!

And what about the Piper? He had let me down too. Hadn't he promised me this special land? Hadn't he filled my eyes and ears and thoughts with pictures of the promised land? Hadn't he led me right up to the door of it and then *"Bang!"* shut the door in my face? Hadn't he left me feeling alone, neither belonging here nor belonging there? Where was he now? It seems once he put us here he lost interest. He just used us to make our parents suffer. He didn't really want us.

And the friends, the children? Were they any better? They'd left me behind, left me out and then they'd simply forgotten me. Now they've even forgotten they forgot me! I felt a terrible, desperate bitterness and loneliness. There was no one to rely on.

I lay back and sank into a cloud, remembering. Remembering how I'd felt as I waited for the party that never happened. Remembering the grown ups shuffling away, sad-eyed and guilty-looking. I could see their faces in my mind. I could see now how bad they'd felt about letting me down. I had been blinded by my own disappointment at the time. Now I remembered Ben's touch on my shoulder, a slight embarrassed touch, shy of a hug, and the gruffly muttered, "Try to forgive them, lad. Try to understand."

Maybe I was beginning to understand. That day on Koppelberg Hill I had been flooded by feelings. They swept me away and I washed up here. I had been carried along. But now I could think and understand and choose. I could decide where I wanted to be.

I understood now that everyone lets you down sometime and they always would. Probably I would let others down in my turn. But now I felt I was beginning to understand the how and the why and I could forgive. Grown ups made mistakes. Why expect them to be perfect?

This land I was in now was perfect but it felt perfectly unreal and unsatisfying. A land without shadows. A land of plenty. It was like drowning in treacle. I almost longed to suck a sharp sour lemon for refreshment, just to make a change. You need a bit of sour to appreciate the sweet I realised.

Thoughtfully, I climbed back down to the valley.

26
— Word pictures —

These trips up to the in-between became more and more precious to me. I stopped wanting to merge in, to forget and be comfortable. I began to treasure my difference.

My rememberings and thinkings enriched my stories, helping to bring them to life. I could describe things I remembered so well that you could almost see and smell them. I made word pictures; pictures of market day in Hamelin – the colours of the fruit stands in the sunshine, the scent of strawberries ripening. I tried to conjure up the sounds of everyday life – the bustlings, the clatterings, the chattering. I described our homes so well you could almost feel the warm fires glowing, smell the cakes baking. I told all sorts of stories; fairy stories and scary stories, silly stories, sad stories, beautiful and terrible stories, tales of tragedy and humiliation, stories of monsters and gods, lost children, stories of magic, stories of love, stories of battles.

With each story a little more colour crept into a few more faces. I added concrete to their cotton-wool world. I told of worlds that had darkness as well as light, old as well as young, happiness and sadness, light and shade instead of a permanent twilight.

I spoke of the school house, the church, the people. I spoke of the shepherd we called Old Ben. Ben, who always seemed more old-fashioned than the other parents. Ben, with his bluff kindness, his understanding, his tenderness and care for his sheep. Ben, who, after all these years, was still wandering on the hillside looking for Rosie and Max ...

"I want to go home," said Rosie.

She surprised everyone. She surprised herself.

"Oh!" she said, and put her hand to her mouth, amazed at what she had said, as if it had just slipped out. Then, her eyes grey and thoughtful, she repeated, "I do want to go home. I want to see Dad and the sheep."

Next to her, Max looked astonished as if someone had shaken him up from a long sleep and he didn't quite know where he was yet.

Then, "I want to go home too," said Janie.

"Me too," said Peter.

"And me ..."

"And me ..."

Then the wailing started, as when babies wake and wail. It built up and went from one to the other, building, building, their dream eyes changing to tears, their fantasies changing to memories. Their eyes wide, their mouths open, the noise growing from wailing to sobbing to shouting and chattering. A sense of spells being broken, of life flooding in.

27
— Plans —

All that night we talked, we remembered, we planned, we imagined and we wondered.

"How long have we been here?"

"Will the Piper let us go?"

"Is he still here or has he just left us here?"

"Don't you think we've paid the price – made up for the broken promise?"

"How did we get here?"

"I sort of melted into the mountain," I said. "It was as if I wanted it so badly that it happened."

"My mind was just full of pictures of in here," said Martha. "I sort of floated in here on a dream."

"So," said Peter, becoming more like his old bossy self, "we could get out the same way. Easy."

"Not that easy!" I say. "Climbing the cloud bank is difficult. You have to concentrate really hard. Fill your head with outside thoughts. Don't listen to the pipes ..."

"We can stuff our ears with moss," said Martha.

"We'd look pretty stupid," said Max.

"Who cares," said Martha, "if it helps us to get back. You do want to go back don't you?"

Max didn't look so sure.

"'Course he does!" said Rosie. "And I've got another idea. Why don't we make our own music, sing our own songs."

We were still chattering and singing and wondering and remembering as we stood up and, one by one, helped each other to

start the climb. Hand in hand, we went. Each following the one in front. And in front of the whole line of children there was I, leading the way.

"Ugh, I'm sinking!" shouted Janie, as her foot squelched into the cloud bank.

"Don't sink. Think!" said Rosie. "Think of your house, your family. Think of your own room, your bed and sing with me. Sing along."

A sudden surge up!

"That's the way," I encouraged. "Think home!" I shouted.

"Think mother!" shouted Martha.

"And father!" said Peter.

"And – pets ..."

"... and toys and ..."

On and on, up and up.

Suddenly a doubt clouded my mind. What if I became like the Piper? What if I led them up here with thoughts and visions and then left someone behind, lost and abandoned?

We all slip backwards a bit and I look down.

A long way down, there is Max. He has stopped. His eyes are dreamy and he's gazing back down the valley. He's going to slide back. Is he going to pull us back with him?

28
— Hamelin spring —

In Hamelin, the cobbled streets sparkle faintly in the early spring sunshine. Window boxes are sunny with daffodils. The townsfolk are gathering in the church for their Easter Sunday service. They shuffle and cough and look towards the stained-glass window behind the pulpit. The window is another memorial to the disappeared. On it, in rainbow colours, stiff little figures are forever frozen in mid-skip. A long line of stained-glass children, forever skipping and climbing up the mountain. At the bottom of the window, their names are etched in black – Jacob and Mary, Rosie and Max, Peter and Martha and Alice and Janie and Rebecca and Daisy and Rachel and Sarah and Tom ... The church artist has made a start on the faint outline of the last name – Joseph.

The minister steps into the pulpit.

"We are gathered here today to celebrate the Easter Rising and to pray once more that we may be forgiven and our children returned to us. Let us pray."

The townsfolk pray fiercely, eyes tight, hands clenched.

"Let us now sing hymn number 416 – 'Sing of Springtime'."

The congregation clear their throats and rise to sing:

"Now the winter days are over,
Spring is rising, hope is too.
For our children we implore you,
Return them and we'll sin no more.

> *We see all around us rise.*
> *We rejoice in earth and skies*
> *And we offer up our sighs.*
> *Return our children we implore."*

"MAX!" screams Rosie. "He's getting left behind."

I feel her loosening her grip on my hand and being drawn back down. I try to hang on to her and pull her along but she slides away and I'm left up here, my hand still raised and clenched as if I'm waving to her.

Janie turns round and stares. Her round eyes begin to fill with the dream stare she has so recently lost. I feel a sinking sensation as I watch her slither. I grab hold of her before she slides.

"We've got to carry on!" I shout to her and to all the others. "Think Hamelin. Think mother. Think home ..."

We carry on chanting, singing, struggling, scrambling.

Behind us, Rosie and Max are becoming little dots in the distance. Is it my imagination or do I still hear Rosie's clear high voice singing?

> *"Spring in Hamelin,*
> *Meadows bright.*
> *Showers and sunshine*
> *Streaming bright."*

It sounds like a ghostly echo from far away.

29
— Chill wind —

I shiver.

"Can you feel it too?" asks Martha.

"What?"

"Fresh air. Spring air!"

And yes, "I can feel it!"

"I feel it too!" yells Peter.

"And me!"

"And me!"

"We're very close now!" I shout. "Shut out the Piper's music and think and sing of Hamelin.

> *Sing of Hamelin*
> *With all your might.*
> *Showers and sunshine*
> *Streaming bright."*

Singing, shouting, thinking, hoping, scrambling, pulling, pushing and then a watery beam of sunlight is inching through from somewhere. It sparkles in the air, revealing a myriad dancing dust motes. Then a creaking, an opening and ... light. It's bright and clear and dazzling. The air is chill, the grass damp and fresh, the sky immense above us.

We blink.

"Is this it?" asks Martha. "Have we made it?"

30
— The real world —

"It's cold," says Peter. "Windy."

"And so big," says Janie. "Frightening."

"You get used to it," I say.

"It's wet," she says. "Look!" and she points to a marshy patch of grass.

"Puddles!" says Peter. "I remember puddles!" and he splashes his big foot in it. Shrieks of surprise and delight from some who join in, jumping, splashing, rolling around like puppies.

Others stand uncertain, like Janie, and shiver ...

"I'm scared," she whines. "I can hear ghosts. Listen."

On the air comes a long eerie sound:

"Waaaaaaaa."

I've heard that sound before. What is it? I'm still trying to remember when, over the brow of the hill, comes a straggle of sheep. Of course!

"It's just sheep," I say, "bleating – and look! There's Ben!"

He's rubbing his eyes and muttering.

"'Tain't possibly them ..." he's saying. "Trick of the light."

He stares at us as if we are ghosts and I begin to wonder, "Have we really arrived or are we still on the edge, ready to slip either way?"

I feel faint, ready to fall. Janie is huddling back against the stone and grass of the mountain. She is ready to give in and fade back into the mountain. We stare at him. I need him to believe in us but he just stands and rubs his eyes.

Then another sound floats towards us. A thin, reedy, tired sound. It's Rosie, still singing bravely and struggling up.

> *"Green grass blowing,*
> *Clear air blowing*
> *And we are knowing*
> *Spring is here ..."*

She sounds muffled and distant and her voice is wavering but, even so, Ben catches the sound and "Rosie!" he screams, "Max!" and he's running and shouting and laughing and crying and we're smiling and singing too – singing together to help Rosie and Max. Our own fears forgotten, we join in with Rosie.

And Ben stands there, his face breaking into smiles, his arms open, ready to hug his long-lost children.

Down in Hamelin the service is drawing to a close. The sun has risen now and pours through the window, dappling small fragments of rainbow on to the people. The organist, her arms held up in the air, is ready to bring her hands down on the keys for the final hymn. The congregation coughs and takes a communal breath, ready to sing, when voices from outside come wafting in. The people shuffle and look at each other, "What?"

A man at the back opens the big church doors and peers out nervously. Mrs Slater is hobbling to the door, her curiosity stronger than her fear and her hope strongest of all. Others stand and turn around, some are clutching at each other, holding their breath. They don't dare to believe. Joseph's mother is at the door now too. She's shaking so badly she can hardly stand.

"Can you hear it, Jack?" she whispers to her husband. He's afraid to reply, afraid to hope.

Then Ben comes into view. He seems twenty years younger. He's running! And he's holding Rosie by one hand and Max by the other. All three of them are pink and windswept and wreathed in smiles.

"Believe it! Believe it!" he's yelling and behind him is the strangest sight. Joseph, marching proud and tall, next to Peter and Martha. And there's Janie skipping along and Tom and Rebecca and Jacob and Mary and Alice and Daisy, Will and John and Rachel and Sarah and Rob and all the lost children.

Some are walking stiff and uncertain, others are running and tumbling. Some are rolling down the hillside like Easter eggs.

Here they are, a ragbag of rainbow-tattered, mud-splattered, rosy, laughing, singing children coming home.

Coming home at last.